THE Deep River COLLECTION

Ten Spirituals arranged for Solo Voice and Piano

by Moses Hogan

T0034092

Cover photo by Emery Clark

ISBN 978-0-634-02116-9

HAL•LEONARD®
CORPORATION
7777 W. BLUEMOUND RD. P.O. BOX 13819 MILWAUKEE, WI 53213

Visit Hal Leonard Online at
www.halleonard.com

FOREWORD:

In a time and place where physical hardship and emotional anguish were a way of life for a people in bondage, God placed into their hearts and onto their lips a song. So powerful was this song that in its words was hope itself, in its melody the peace for which their hearts yearned, and in its rhythm the pulse of the Almighty who sustained them. That song was the spiritual, and it survives to this day as one of the most deeply moving expressions of the human spirit.

The spirituals were first sung by individuals whose names we can never know. The anonymity of their authors, however, adds to the poignancy of these songs, for it leaves us to imagine the kind of suffering that pressed such music from their souls. In the words of the spirituals are expressed the deep longings and the naked faith of people kept by design from formal education. Their words, then, are necessarily simple and direct, conveying the most fervent desires for freedom and family, for peace and prosperity, through unpolished dialect and biblical images.

The melodies of the spirituals likewise possess the haunting beauty that has simplicity as its handmaid. But in their simplicity is hidden a degree of harmonic sophistication that was left for subsequent generations of arrangers and composers to explore. Europeans such as Dvořák found in the spirituals a wealth of melodic material upon which to base symphonic compositions, but fittingly, it was a group of African-American composers and conductors who pioneered the art of arranging the spirituals for solo and choral performance. In the hands of early masters such as Harry T. Burleigh and Hall Johnson, the spirituals retained their lyrical directness and their emotional power while taking on a new measure of harmonic refinement.

It is upon the foundation established by these pioneers that Moses Hogan has built, adding his own unique contribution to the deep river of the Negro spirituals. As is evident in the songs of the Deep River collection, in his work are fused the harmonic sensibility honed by his years as a student and practitioner of classical piano literature, his love of the human voice, and his musical roots in the African-American Baptist church.

In honor of Edna Sampson Hargett
Commissioned by The Negro Spiritual Scholarship Foundation for the
1999 GRADY-RAYAM PRIZE IN SACRED MUSIC, Orlando, Florida

Deep River

Based on Joshua 3

Traditional Spiritual
Arranged by MOSES HOGAN

Dedicated to Marietta Simpson

He Never Said a Mumbalin' Word
(Crucifixion)

Traditional Spiritual
Arranged by MOSES HOGAN

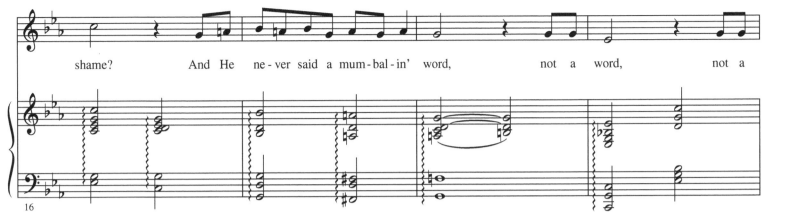

shame? And He ne - ver said a mum - bal - in' word, not a word, not a

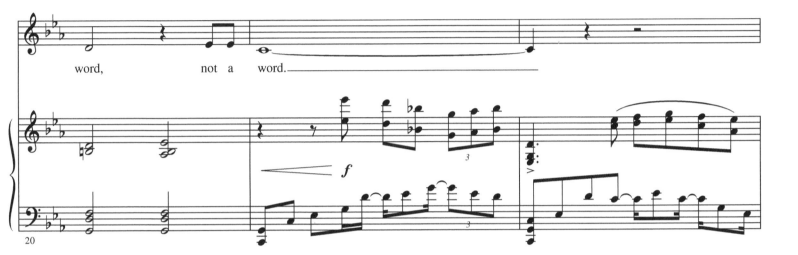

word, not a word.

rall.

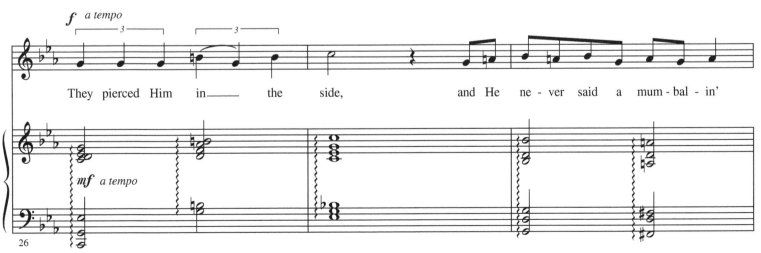

f *a tempo*

They pierced Him in the side, and He ne - ver said a mum - bal - in'

mf *a tempo*

word. They pierced Him in——— the side, and He

ne - ver said a mum - bal - in' word, not a word, not a word, not a

Unhurried

word.

Ped. Ped.

His blood came trick - ling

Ped. Ped.

He bowed His head___ and died, and He nev-er said a mum-bal-in'

word. He bowed His head___ and died, and He

nev-er said a mum-bal-in' word, not a word, not a

Slower to end

portamento

word, not a word.___

L.H.   R.H. _dim._   L.H.   R.H.

ppp

Ped.   Ped.

Dedicated to Mr. John and Jeanne Green

Give Me Jesus

Traditional Spiritual
Arranged by MOSES HOGAN

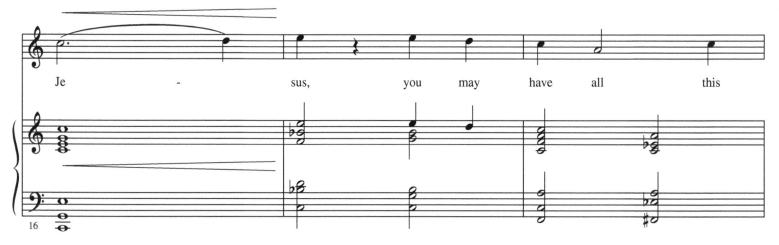

Je - sus, you may have all this

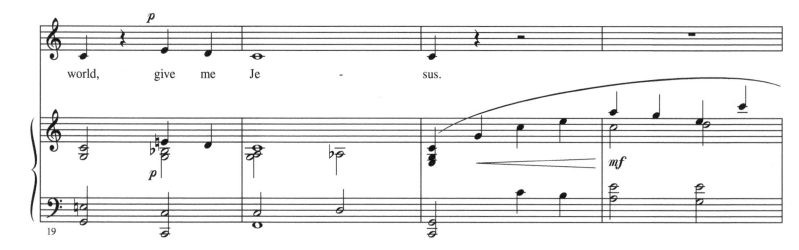

world, give me Je - sus.

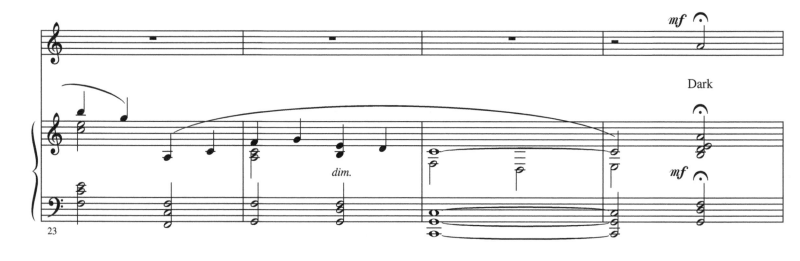

Dark

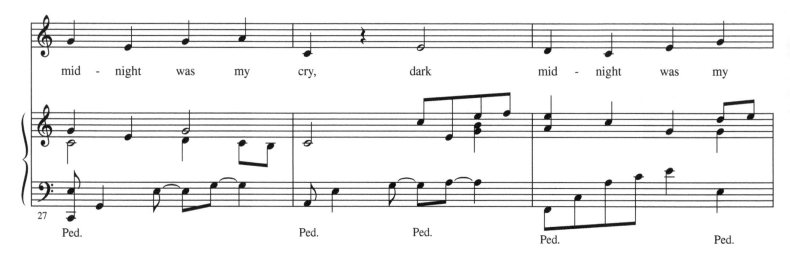

mid - night was my cry, dark mid - night was my

Ped.   Ped.   Ped.   Ped.   Ped.

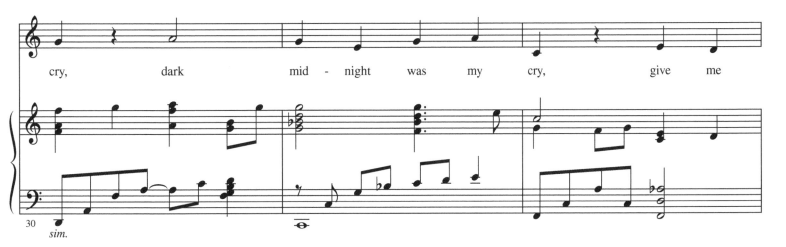

cry, dark mid-night was my cry, give me

Je - sus. Give me Je -

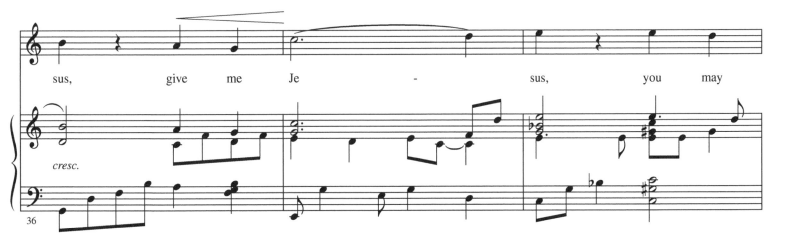

sus, give me Je - sus, you may

have all___ of this___ world, give me Je -

14

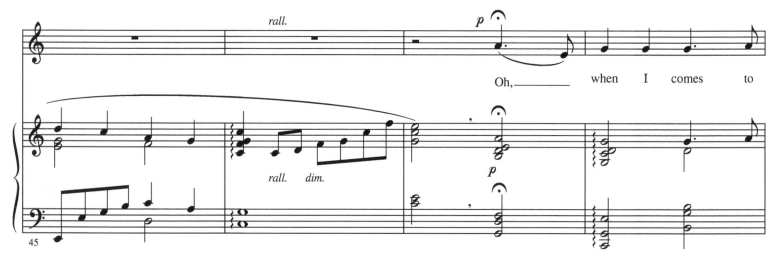

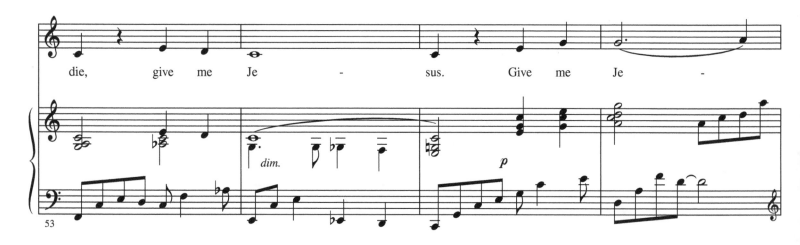

sus, no-bo-dy but Je - sus, you may have all___ of this___ world, give me Je - sus.

No-bo-dy but Je - sus, oh,___ you may have all___ of this___ world, give me Je - sus.

Dedicated to Jo Ann and Joshua Stovall

He's Got the Whole World in His Hands

Traditional Spiritual
Arranged by MOSES HOGAN

whole world___ in His hands, He's got the whole world in His hands.___
all the pow - er in His hands, He's got the

He's got___

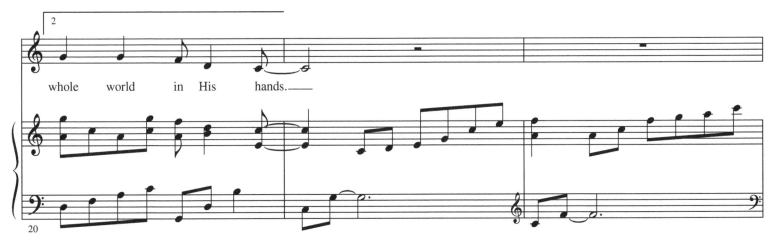

whole world in His hands.___

He's got you and me, broth - er,

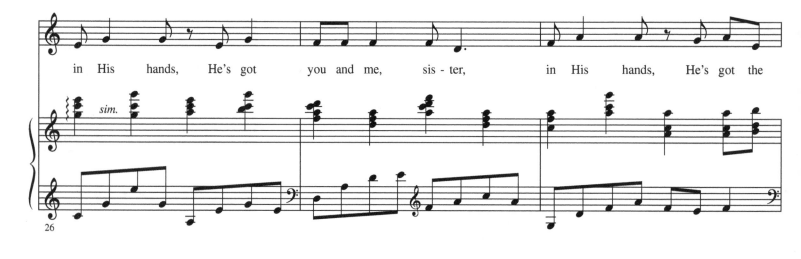

in His hands, He's got you and me, sis - ter, in His hands, He's got the

lit - tle ba - by in His hands, He's got the whole world in His hands.

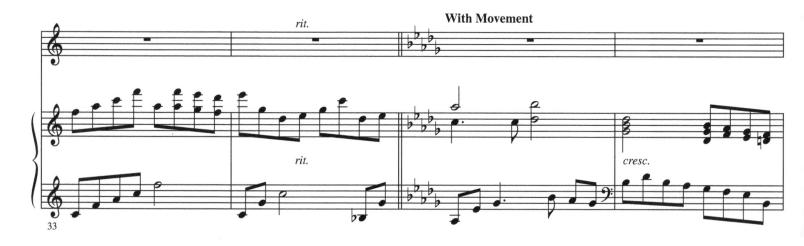

rit. **With Movement**

rit. *cresc.*

Dedicated to Brian Stratton

Let Us Break Bread Together

Traditional Spiritual
Arranged by MOSES HOGAN

Moderato, with feeling

Let us break bread to-geth-er on our knees, _____

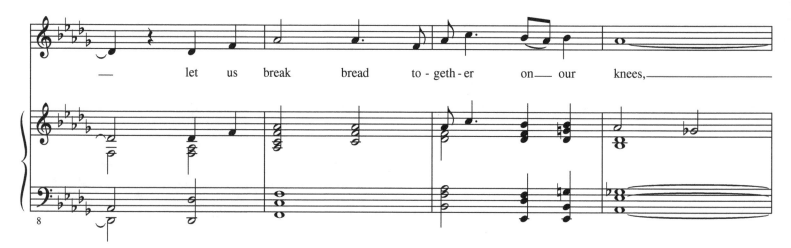

— let us break bread to-geth-er on our knees, _____

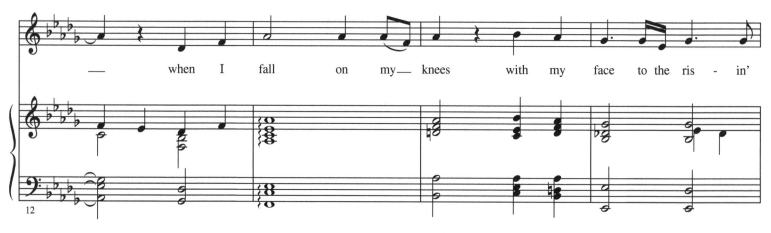

— when I fall on my knees with my face to the ris - in'

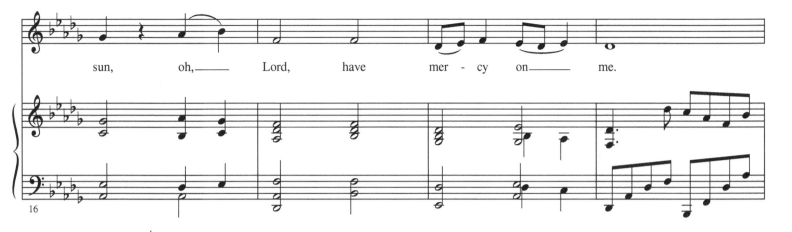

sun, oh,____ Lord, have mer - cy on____ me.

Let us drink wine to - geth - er on____ our

knees,_____ let us drink wine to -

geth - er on____ our knees,_____ when I

fall on my knees with my face to the ris - in'

sun, oh, Lord, have mer - cy on

Broaden *f*

me. Let us praise God to -

geth - er on our knees, let us

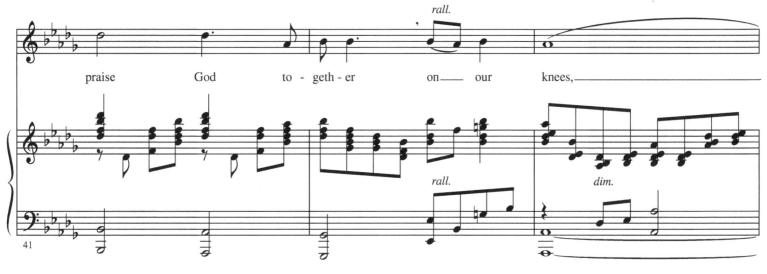

praise God to-geth-er on our knees,

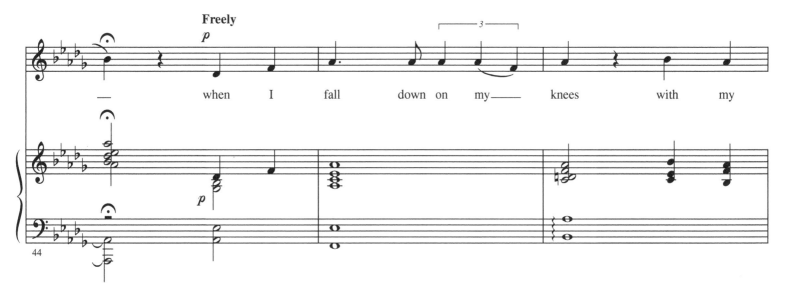

Freely

when I fall down on my knees with my

face to the ris - in' sun, oh, Lord, have

mer - cy on me

Dedicated to Derek Lee Ragin

My Good Lord's Done Been Here

Traditional Spiritual
Arranged by MOSES HOGAN

Moderato, with joy!

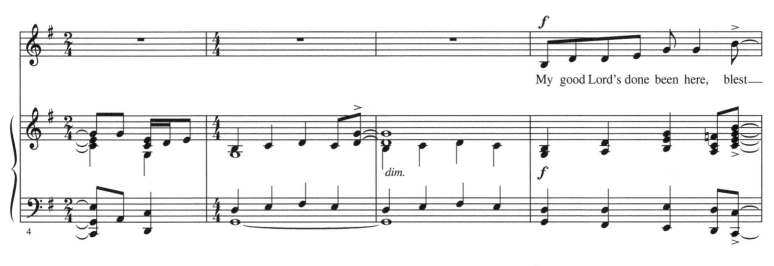

My good Lord's done been here, blest—

— my soul,— and gone a-way. My good Lord's done been here, blest——— my soul,— and—

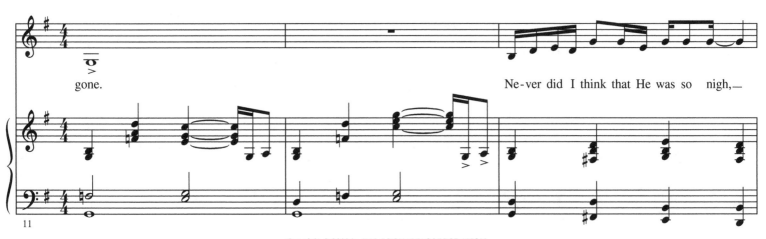

gone.

Ne-ver did I think that He was so nigh,—

blest my soul,— and gone; He spoke— and He made me— laugh and cry,—

blest my soul— and— gone. My good Lord's done been here, blest— my soul,— and gone a-way.

My good Lord's done been here, blest— my soul,— and— gone.

Sin-ner bet-ter min' how you walk on the cross,— blest my soul— and— gone; your

foot— might— slip and your soul get lost,— blest my soul,— and— gone. My good Lord's done been here, blest—

— my soul,— and gone a-way. My good Lord's done— been here, blest— my soul,— and— gone.

Broaden

My good Lord's done been here, blest— my soul,— and gone a-way. My—— good Lord's done been here, and He

blest my soul,— blest my soul,— blest my soul— and— gone.—————

Dedicated to Dr. Andre Thomas

Somebody's Knockin' at Yo' Door

Traditional Spiritual
Arranged by MOSES HOGAN

Some - bod - y's knock - in' at yo' door,_____

some - bod - y's knock - in' at yo' door._____

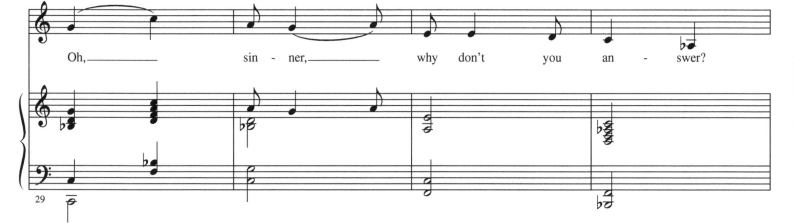

Oh,_____ sin - ner,_____ why don't you an - swer?

Some - bod - y's knock - in' at yo' door.

Freely, reflective   *(repeat twice to m. 21)*

Can't you hear_____ Him?
Sounds like Je - sus.
Je - sus calls_____ you.

Dedicated to Alfred Walker

Sometimes I Feel Like a Motherless Child

Traditional Spiritual
Arranged by MOSES HOGAN

home.

Some-times I feel like I'm al - mos' gone,—— some-times I feel like I'm

al - mos' gone,—— some-times I feel—— like I'm al - mos' gone,—— a

_f_

mf legato

cresc.

R.H.

R.H.

long   ways,—   a long   ways,—

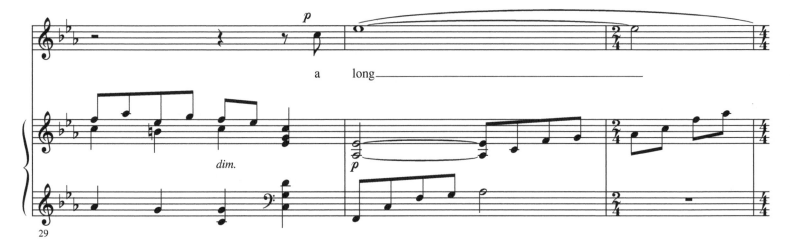

a   long————————

ways————   from   home.————————

Dedicated to Dr. Benjamin Harlan

Were You There?

Traditional Spiritual
Arranged by MOSES HOGAN

trem - ble,   trem - ble. Were you there   when they   cru - ci - fied   my

With Movement

Lord?   Were   you

mp legato

Ped.   Ped.   Ped.   Ped.   Ped.

there   when they   laid Him in   the   tomb?_____   Were   you

sim.

there   when they   laid Him in   the   tomb?_____

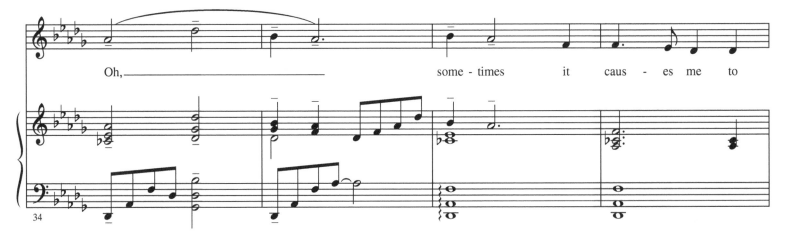

Oh,_____ some - times it caus - es me to

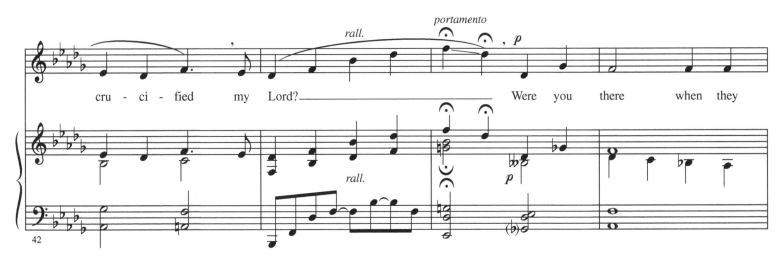

trem - ble, trem - ble, trem - ble. Were you there when they

cru - ci - fied my Lord?_____ Were you there when they

cru - ci - fied my Lord?_____

Dedicated to Bridget Bazile

Walk Together Children

Traditional Spiritual
Arranged by MOSES HOGAN

Oh,— walk to - geth - er child - ren, *don't— you get wea - ry,

walk to - geth - er child - ren, don't— you get wea - ry, walk to - geth - er child - ren, don't—

— you get wea - ry, there's a great camp - meet - in' in the pro - mised lan'. Oh,—

* Don't you = pronounced "don'tcha"

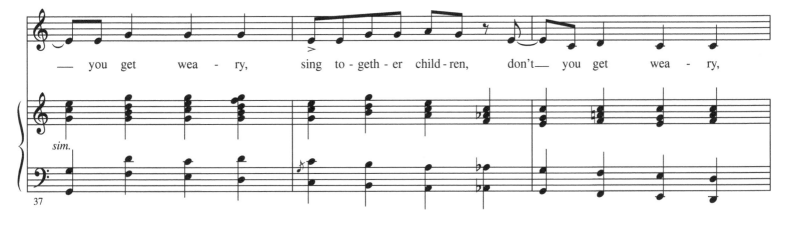

you get wea - ry, sing to - geth - er child - ren, don't you get wea - ry,

shout to - geth - er child - ren, don't you get wea - ry, there's a

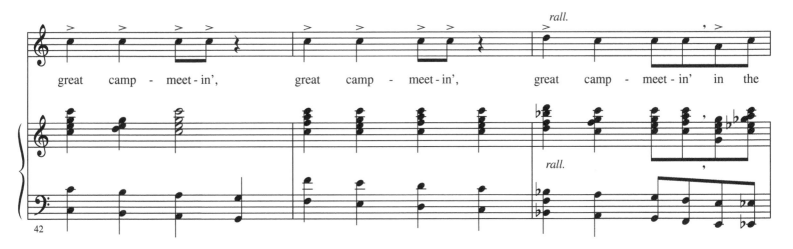

great camp - meet - in', great camp - meet - in', great camp - meet - in' in the

pro - mised, pro - mised lan'.

BIOGRAPHY

MOSES GEORGE HOGAN (1957-2003) was born in New Orleans, Louisiana. A pianist, conductor and arranger of international renown, he was a graduate of the New Orleans Center for Creative Arts (NOCCA) and Oberlin Conservatory of Music in Ohio. He also studied at New York's Julliard School of Music and Louisiana State University in Baton Rouge. Mr. Hogan's many accomplishments as a concert pianist included winning first place in the prestigious 28th annual Kosciuszko Foundation Chopin Competition in New York.

Mr. Hogan's discography includes a recording of arrangements of spirituals for the acclaimed soprano Barbara Hendricks, sung by the Moses Hogan Singers, entitled *Give Me Jesus,* produced by EMI Virgin Records; *An American Heritage of Spirituals,* sung by the famed Mormon Tabernacle Choir, conducted by Moses Hogan and Albert McNeil; two recordings of spirituals with renowned countertenor Derek Lee Ragin on Aria and on Channel Classics Records; the 1995 PBS Documentary, *The American Promise,* whose soundtrack was released separately by Windham Hill Records under the title *Voices;* and the newly released *Moses Hogan Vocal and Choral Series* which includes the complete works of Mr. Hogan conducted and produced by Moses Hogan, sung by the acclaimed Moses Hogan Singers on MGH Records. Hogan's contemporary settings of spirituals and other works have become staples in the repertoires of high school, college, church, community and professional choirs and have been revered by audiences and praised by critics worldwide. Hogan's compositions and arrangements are available exclusively through Hal Leonard Corporation.

For more information about the complete recorded arrangements of Mr. Hogan, sung by the Moses Hogan Singers and conducted by Mr. Hogan, contact:

Hal Leonard Corporation
7777 W. Bluemound Road
Milwaukee, WI 53213
www.halleonard.com

For a complete listing of choral and solo works by Moses Hogan published exclusively by Hal Leonard, contact the Publisher or your favorite music retailer.